this little piggy

this little piggy

A celebration of the world's most irresistible pet

Jane Croft

Photography by Kate Whitaker
Kyle Cathie Limited

For my Mum
who put up with my very first micro pig in her house. Thanks Mum – I love you x

First published in Great Britain in 2010 by
Kyle Cathie Limited
23 Howland Street
London W1T 4AY
general.enquiries@kyle-cathie.com
www.kylecathie.com

10 9 8 7 6 5 4 3 2 1

ISBN 978-1-85626-960-5

Project editor: Catharine Robertson
Designer: Smith & Gilmour
Photographer: Kate Whitaker
Copy editor: Ruth Baldwin
Production: Gemma John

A Cataloguing In Publication record for this title is available from the British Library.

Colour reproduction by Sang Choy, Singapore
Printed and bound in China by C&C Offset Printing Company Ltd.

Contents

Introduction

Introduction

I am passionate about animals. They are as important to me as any human being — and frequently much better company! Working with animals is the only thing I've ever wanted to do. Sadly, it never paid the bills. So I've had jobs in the city and travelled the world, but nothing ever felt quite right. I always had one elegant foot in the business world and the other desperate to get into a wellington boot out in the fresh air.

Years ago I went on a pig-keeping course, just out of interest, and bought a couple of Kune Kunes to keep in my garden. They were gorgeous — friendly, cuddly and fun. But they were *big*. Fully grown, Enoch, the boar, was large enough for me to ride him around the garden. I definitely couldn't let them into the kitchen for treats once they had grown to their full beautiful size.

These two needed a home of their own with more outside space. I rented some land for this purpose and also began breeding Gloucester Old Spots on a very small scale. It was no more than a tiny cottage industry, my idea being to provide the village pub with locally sourced meat. On paper it made sense, but unfortunately I had omitted to factor in my natural tendency to form a relationship with an animal and become totally besotted. I gave my pigs names, cared for them and grew so attached to each one

that I simply couldn't bear the thought of sending them off to be butchered.

Then my mum fell ill and I moved back home to Essex to care for her. There was no possibility of taking the pigs with me. With a heavy heart I gave my beautiful Kune Kunes to a children's petting farm where I'm glad to report they are leading extremely happy lives. But I pined for my pigs. I missed the way they would charge at high speed to greet me in the mornings. I missed their extraordinary intelligence and empathy. Most of all, I missed lying down in their quarters at night, snug and warm between their bodies, which were like giant hot-water bottles.

As my mother slowly began to improve, I spent my evenings researching pigs and breeders. A website of a farm with miniature pigs seemed to answer all my needs, and I realised that for the first time in my life I might be able to start my own business, one which – if you'll excuse the pun – would bring home the bacon as well as fulfilling my dream to be involved with some of the most affectionate animals there are. There was just one problem. The pigs were only readily available from the USA. I began to scour the UK looking for tiny pigs and, a year later, I bought my first micro pig. I named her Hope and brought her home.

Mum initially hated the idea of a pig in the house; she thought pigs were dirty, messy animals. She was soon proved wrong. Hope was fastidious about her personal hygiene, sweet-natured and immediately bonded with my dog Daisy. They became inseparable, sleeping together at night in a basket under the stairs. Once I'd put child locks on the fridge to prevent uninvited foraging, I can honestly say that living with my pet pig was a total joy for us all. It was a good start. I was more determined than ever to breed these wonderful creatures so that others could also experience the pleasure of bringing up a pet pig for themselves.

When Mum was well enough for me to leave her, I moved to Cambridgeshire where I began to build up my herd. The first litter was born in October 2009. Our local newspaper came to take photographs and the story made it to the front page. A week later, my piglets were in the national press. They were also on BBC1's *News at Ten* and live on NBC's *Today Show* in New York via a satellite link to my farm. Journalists flocked to my door. I was inundated with requests to appear on more TV and radio programmes.

I always knew that people would fall in love with micro pigs.

It was then I realised my instincts had been spot on. Micro pigs touched hearts. I always knew that, like me, other people would fall in love with them. What I hadn't expected or planned for was that, virtually overnight, my Little Pig Farm, as I named it, had gone global. Never had the phrase 'Where there's muck there's money' been more true. Each little pig costs between £500 and £1,200. The phone never stops ringing and my waiting list of potential owners is huge. Perhaps I wasn't so bonkers after all!

History and breeding

History

Pigs have been thriving for 40 million years and are one of the most widespread mammals on the planet — they live on every continent in the world except Antarctica.

At any one time there are about 1 billion pigs in the world.

Pigs were domesticated around 7,000 BC, and are now the top meat-producing animals on earth.

But they're not simply a source of delicious pork, ham and bacon. For some time now scientists have been aware that the pig is the smartest animal in the farmyard. Their brains are similar to, but smaller than, those of humans, which means they are intelligent, can express emotions and have the capacity to problem-solve. Laboratory tests have proved their intelligence to be so high that they can quickly work out problems as fast as, or even faster than, chimps.

HISTORY AND BREEDING

Pigs were the first animals

ever to be used domestically.

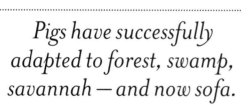

Pigs have successfully adapted to forest, swamp, savannah — and now sofa.

Much more recently micro pigs have been happy to make themselves at home in urban gardens and domestic kitchens, cuddling up with other pets and their owners on the family sofa. Pet pigs were once as improbable as the pink flying variety, but not any more. With their cartoon faces and playful natures, big-hearted little micro pigs have a worldwide fan base and are top of the pet wish list. In a word, they are irresistible. What's not to love?

Breeding

In the mid-1980s small pot-bellied pigs were introduced to the USA. They were brought over from Vietnam by soldiers who had fallen for their intelligence and charms. Instinctively, they thought they would make great pets. The movie star George Clooney is one of the most famous pot-bellied pig owners. Max, his 135kg (300lb) pet, lived with Clooney for eighteen years. He had been a wonderful and much loved companion who, in 1996, reputedly woke up Clooney just before an earthquake.

George Clooney said he enjoyed the longest relationship of his life with his pig, and they sometimes even shared a bed.

This 'third sense' in pigs has been well reported. Another American pot-bellied pet was with his owner in a fairly remote cabin when the man became seriously ill. The pig took off to the nearest road where he lay down so that he could stop the traffic and somehow summon help. Pigs are loyal and they have a good memory. You don't ever want to be mean to a pig. Love them and they will love you back unconditionally.

An average small pot-bellied pig weighs 30–70kg (70–150lb) and is approximately 1m (40in) long and 30cm (12in) tall. Some of the largest — like Clooney's Max — can be double that. This is still small compared to a domestic pig, which can grow to anything between 270–900kg (600–2,000lb).

Gradually, small pot-bellied pigs were brought to Europe. Over the subsequent twenty years they have been bred with other pigs — Kune Kunes, Tamworths and Gloucester Old Spots. The result is the modern micro pig, which comes in all shapes, sizes and colours.

A true micro pig should be no taller than 40–45cm (15–18in), which is roughly knee height.

Sadly, as soon as pot-bellied pigs became very popular in the USA, some unscrupulous breeders sold piglets that were not true miniatures. Innocent customers ended up with huge animals crashing around their homes. If you want to make sure that your little pig really is a little pig, it's important to buy from a reputable breeder.

Can I have one?

Piglets

Breeders have to rely on their experience and the size of the parent pigs when predicting how big their offspring might become. No one can guarantee the actual size of your pig when it is fully grown.

Here's a rough guide: at their largest they should compare in size to a dog such as a Labrador or Mastiff. The smallest ones will be the size of a Cocker Spaniel. Their colouring may be black, white, ginger, brown or pink with spots and splashes of different shades. Quite often piglets from the same litter will have completely different markings and colours from each other.

As I write this, one of my splendid pigs, Humbug, is feeding her litter of eight tiny black piglets which were born yesterday. Humbug, as her name suggests, is the colour of a humbug. Her piglets couldn't wait to have their photographs taken for the book!

Each pig seems to grow into its name, so it's worth spending time thinking up something which will go with its personality. Popular names include Babe, Rodney, Wilbur, Chops and Peppa. My newest pet is Lady Gaga, who at four weeks old is already showing signs of becoming a superstar.

Watching baby piglets come into the world is a very special privilege. Nature never ceases to astound me. The piglets are born with teeth and already able to walk. They can find their way to a teat with no problem at all. Once a piglet has chosen a teat, it becomes its own: no matter how many piglets are in a litter, they always go back to the same teat.

Every micro pig is an individual and, just like people, they will vary in weight, height, colouring and personality.

Commitment

A micro pig is a long-term commitment, given that its lifespan is anything from ten to fifteen years. Your micro pig is going to become a member of the family. As a breeder, I want my pigs to go to the best possible homes. Before I will even consider allowing anyone to buy one of my pigs, I ask a lot of questions. I must be sure that the new home will include a big enough garden, and I have to know that the owners are not going to be out all day. If they work or have other commitments, someone needs to be available to make sure the pig is fed regularly and let in and out of the house.

Unlike dogs, pigs don't need to be taken for walks. As far as exercise goes, they are happy to wander in a good-sized garden. Another big plus for having a pig as a pet is that as their skin is very similar to human skin — they have hair rather than fur. Unlucky people who are allergic to dogs and cats can happily be in the company of a pig without suffering from watery eyes, a runny nose or constant sneezing. I have never come across anyone who is allergic to pigs. And with no fur to shed, pigs are also low-maintenance: no more animal hair on furniture and carpets.

A pig's sense of smell is so well developed it can easily find things underground.

Things to consider

REGULATIONS

In the UK there are very strict rules that you must adhere to when considering having pigs in your life. These rules are very important and have been put in place to avoid diseases being spread.

Firstly you must apply for a County Parish Holding number. These can be obtained free of charge from your local Animal Health Office (see p.93). This is a licence to keep livestock on your land or premises. You cannot own a pig until this has been allocated.

When you get your pig home it must stay on the property or land that the CPH number was allocated to. You can't put your pig in the car and take it to see your friends or family. You can only move your pig to another location if that too has a CPH number. Even then you have to fill in a movement form and send it to Animal Health, and the pig must stay a minimum of 21 days at that property.

The only exception to this is if you take your pig to the vet for medical attention. You also cannot walk your pig unless you have a special Walking Licence issued by Animal Health. But as long as they have enough room in your garden, taking pigs for long walks is not recommended.

If you don't live in the UK you need to check your country's regulations.

VETERINARIAN

It's vital to have a vet nearby who can treat your pet if it gets sick or requires inoculations. You will need to register with a well-respected large-animal or farm vet. Check that they are experienced at looking after pigs. Most small-animal vets have little or no experience with pigs.

YOUR PIG'S SIZE

Like all pets, pigs are not just for Christmas or for birthdays. Your adorable baby piglet is going to grow up. Ask the breeder to introduce you to the baby's parents — that will give you some idea of the size you can expect when the piglet is fully adult. Will your house be big enough or would it be better to have a purpose-built pig shelter in the garden?

NEIGHBOURS

Please make absolutely sure that your neighbours will be happy to live next door to a pig (or pigs).

OUTSIDE SPACE

Your pig(s) will need an area of grass where they can root and forage. This needs to be at least 6 x 6m (20 x 20ft). Check that there are no poisonous plants present, such as ferns, ragwort, acorns in large numbers, rhododendron, laburnum, elder, yew and foxgloves: you must not keep a pig in an area with any of these plants.

Allocate a space which your pig can use in warm weather for a good wallow and a place to shelter from the sun.

HOUSING

You will need to build or buy a shelter for your pig if it is not going to live inside. There are lots of fabulous houses on the market now if you're not keen on building one yourself. Some large garden centres sell them or you can look on eBay. Wood is a good material to choose as it is cool in the summer but warm in the winter. There are also new recycled-plastic ones around which can be equally as good. Metal is not recommended as it can be much too warm in summer and too cold in winter. If you are lucky enough to have a stable or brick building/shed, then just make sure that the roof doesn't leak and it is draught-free. For bedding provide plenty of straw. Barley straw makes the best bedding.

Pigs need a constant supply of clean, fresh water. Make sure the water supply is easily accessible.

Pigs are notorious escape artists, so strong, secure fencing is *essential* around all of the outside space. Check it regularly to ensure that there are no gaps or broken parts.

HOLIDAYS

If you go on holiday, who will look after your pig? This is a big consideration as there are no pig equivalents of boarding kennels for dogs and cats. How reliable or trustworthy are the friends or employees you have lined up to cover for you?

Daily care

If you already have a dog or a cat you will know the effort you have to put in to house-train your pets. It requires patience and persistence. You are used to regular feeding, cleaning out litter trays and making sure your pets have enough clean water in their bowls.

Micro pigs are very sociable animals and love the company of other pets, particularly dogs.

Above all you have learned to love your animals and have the pleasure of the love and affection you get back in return. Pigs enjoy company and bond well with other animals, especially dogs. They will follow them around, learning how to behave within the household. Your micro pig, dogs and cats will soon be sharing their baskets, their toys, their bedding and your sofa!

Choosing a pig

Find a reputable breeder. Don't just rely on websites and photographs. Wherever possible, visit the breeder and ask lots of questions. Ask to see the parent pigs to get an idea of how big your little piglet might grow. Get in with the litter and spend time watching their behaviour. You'll soon recognise individual personalities. Pick up the pigs and cuddle them. Some piglets are naturally quite docile and make perfect pets to be around children; others are more mischievous and will keep you on your toes.

Don't be put off by a piglet that squeals — they all do! It's their way of letting us know when they don't like something. Once they feel secure, they should calm down. If a piglet doesn't stop squealing — however appealing it looks — it's probably best to leave that one where it is and choose another. You will instinctively know the one that is just right for you and your family.

It's important to think carefully about the sex of your micro pig. If it is to live as a pet with the family, I would advise buying a castrated boar. Castration neutralises their smell and also calms them down, which makes it easier to discipline and integrate into the home.

Castrated boars make the best household pets.

A gilt is a female pig which has never given birth. Her reproductive cycle begins at four to six months of age. From then on she will come into season every twenty-one days. Don't be surprised when she shows signs of PMT! She might be irritable and moody and leave scent messages around. Be prepared. She can forget her house-training during those hormonal 72 hours and turn into a real nuisance. If you have no intention of breeding, it is far wiser to buy neutered pigs, which make much better family pets.

How many should I get?

It's best to get two micro pigs so that they can keep each other company, if you don't have other pets. They will follow your pets around and can quickly learn how to behave within the household by doing this. Micro pigs will very often learn the rules of toilet training more quickly from their new doggy friends as they follow them in and out of the dog flap or wait by the back door to be let out.

In the wild pigs are never solitary. They bond very well with each other and with other animals.

'*I am very proud to be called a pig. It stands for pride, integrity and guts.*'

–Ronald Reagan

Bringing your pig home

Picking him up

Try to imagine what it feels like to be taken away from your mother and siblings. This is a scary time for piglets. They *hate* to be picked up — their mother never did it. A healthy, aware piglet will scream the place down when first picked up. This is an understandable reaction because, in the wild, piglets can be taken by predators such as large birds. No wonder they are happier when all four trotters are safely on the ground.

Of course, the first thing you will want to do is scoop up your piglet for a cuddle. This is how you do it. Get your piglet used to being on your lap first. Cuddling it and tickling it will give it confidence and relax it. Get it into your arms and stand up slowly. Make sure its feet are on your hand or arm so it thinks it is standing on solid ground. Continue to stroke it and talk to it to make it a pleasurable, not scary experience. Keep the piglet in a quiet, safe, secure place so it can gain confidence and settle happily into unfamiliar surroundings. It won't take long. These little charmers need a lot of TLC, but you will be well rewarded for being gentle and kind.

"'*Piglet*," said Rabbit, taking out a pencil, and licking the end of it, "*you haven't any pluck.*'"

"*It is hard to be brave*," said Piglet, sniffling slightly, "*when you're only a Very Small Animal.*'"

–*Winnie the Pooh*

Preparing your home

Piglets love to nest, so you will need to provide a good sized basket. Before you take your new pet home, have its bed ready with several blankets. Make sure there is a bowl of clean water close by. The bowl must be heavy and sturdy so they don't tip it over.

Try to take some of the straw from your breeder so it has the familiar smells on it. When the piglet gets to your house this will enable it to get used to your smells slowly and not be too confusing.

When you get home, don't just grab your piglet and drag it out of the crate. Try to encourage it with treats or just let it wander out on its own. Do this in a quiet area.

BRINGING YOUR PIG HOME

Bonding

Sit on the floor with your piglet. Talk softly as you would with a baby and any nervousness will soon vanish. Your piglet needs to know you are not a threat. Once trust has been established you will be able to stroke and tickle gently. Pigs love a belly rub!

As soon as you have chosen a name, use it all the time. Piglets can recognise their names by two to three weeks of age and respond when called. When you are starting to instil good behaviour offer little treats. Try using carrot sticks or baby sweetcorn as a reward. You don't want them getting too fat while trying to learn their newest trick! Always praise, tickle and cuddle.

Piglets can learn their own name within a couple of weeks.

Until your piglet is settled, don't leave it alone with any animals in the house or with your children. They will also have to learn what is appropriate behaviour.

Introduce it to other animals slowly. The easiest way is to have your piglet in a crate and let your dog or cat sniff it to get used to the smell. Let them see each other and sniff each other. Remember not to make a huge fuss of your new piglet in front of the other pets as this can encourage jealousy. You can hold it and let the pets come close and sniff. All pigs are individual and some will take to cats and dogs sooner than others. Be patient and it will pay off. Just don't leave your animals alone together in the beginning as it will take time for them to be comfortable with each other and sort out the heirarchy.

You could train them together. If you get your dog to sit and then give him a treat — you could do the same with your pig. That way they both get a treat and there is no favouritism. Don't take your dog's favourite toy and give it to your pig — buy the pig toys and blankets of its own.

Pigs have about 15,000 taste buds — more than any other mammal, including humans.

Making your home pig friendly

Pigs are very inquisitive and will root around anything as tempting as a waste bin at the first opportunity. Empty all reachable cupboards of temptation or make them safe with child locks. Move all house plants, vases and ornaments to above pig height and hide all electrical wires. Make sure your kitchen waste bin is sturdy and locked, or out of the way.

Hope worked out how to open the freezer door just by watching me.

As pigs are both highly intelligent and food-oriented they will figure out a way to get into all but the most secure cupboards. This story about my very first micro pig, Hope, gives some idea of how bright they are, but also what a pain it can be if you're not prepared!

One day when I was living with my mum, I popped out quickly to do some shopping. When I return I was greeted with the sight of Hope sitting in the middle of the kitchen surrounded by semi-frozen peas and garlic bread, and covered from snout to trotters in ice-cream. She had seen me opening the freezer door, remembered how to do it, waited until I had left the house and decided to help herself. My mum was not impressed!

The next time I went out, I fixed a bungee cord from a radiator across the freezer door, but stupidly hooked it onto the handle of a drawer. Hope worked out that if she put her snout under the cord and lifted it, the drawer would open, the cord would slacken off and she could work her way along and still open the door. I came home to a repeat of the first surprise — only this time it was meatballs and garlic bread. You can guess how impressed my mum was!

The third time, I tied a simple knot in the cord, hid and watched. After a while she started to investigate and after another 20 minutes she worked out how to untie the knot. I was very impressed and immediately fitted the child latches that I had bought.

Caring for your pig

Feeding

Regular feeding is important. At Little Pig Farm we feed our pigs at 9am and 5pm. Pigs respond well to routine. They have excellent body clocks and will soon let you know if you are running late! Be vigilant about sturdy water bowls and troughs as your pig grows. Check that there is always clean water, as pigs are thirsty animals.

Your pigs must stick to a vegetarian diet. It should include sow and weaner pellets, which you can buy in bulk from animal feed suppliers, plus plenty of fresh vegetables and fruit. Barley once a week will improve their skin and general wellbeing.

Under DEFRA regulations it is illegal to feed kitchen scraps or peelings to your pig. This is because currently the same rules apply to pet pigs as to pigs bred for meat, and kitchen scraps are classed as processed food. The fruit and vegetables you feed them must not have not passed through your kitchen. Carrots, apples and corn are all huge favourites, but they tend not to like mushrooms or onions. Having said that, every pig is different and you will soon get to know what your pig likes.

In hot weather my pigs love lollies made of peas, carrots and corn frozen in water. I make these in plastic boxes and the pigs enjoy poking at the ice shapes as they melt and reveal the vegetables.

Never give your pigs meat — this is completely unethical. You must also not give them chocolate. Chocolate is poisonous for pigs, just as it is for dogs and other animals. As a special treat I give my pigs Maltesers, but before they can eat them I have to lick off every tiny trace of chocolate — so it's a treat we can share!

Never snack or eat in front of your pig unless you want to share absolutely everything with it. This applies especially to children. Only feed your pig at designated meal times or when training. It may be fun at first to keep giving it treats so that it will be your friend, but it will soon become wearing when you have friends for dinner and your pig is screaming for treats.

Pigs aren't able to look up into the sky.

Grooming

Pigs are very clean animals and love to be groomed. It's also a great way of bonding. I've found that the best thing to use is a rubber studded mitt, which you can buy in most pet shops. It is really good for removing dry skin and smoothing down the hair. The studs massage the skin and increase blood supply.

They also love a good hose down and delight in having a shower with a tiny amount of baby shampoo. Wrap your little pig in a towel after the beauty-parlour treatment and have an extra cuddle. Clean its ears and crevices with cotton wool and warm water.

After their rinse, smooth skin lotion all over your pig's body to help with dry skin. If it's sunny you should use sun lotion as they can burn very easily. But don't use oil-based products as this can 'cook' your pig's skin! Never let them out in the hot sun if there is nowhere for them to shelter.

If your pig gets a cut or scratch you can use honey to help it heal. There really is nothing better for a sore pig. My pig Manuka was very badly burned as a small piglet, but her wounds healed so quickly when I applied Manuka honey to them. Hence the name!

Health

Pigs can catch mange and lice just as cats and dogs catch fleas. They are very easy to get rid of, however. Your pig should be vaccinated against worms and mange every six months. You can use tea tree oil as a natural remedy or you can get a wash or jab from your vet.

Lice can be caught from damp straw or grass. You will be able to see tiny little white eggs in your pig's arm/leg pits and the lice on their bellies. Again you can use tea tree oil or any sort of thick oil – even motor oil will do! I got that tip from a very experienced pig farmer in Kentucky – and it works a treat. Put the oil on the eggs and lice and they fall off.

Pigs can be susceptible to colds and flu, so I vaccinate my pigs against pneumonia. If your pig starts sneezing or coughing take him to the vet immediately. Sometimes they can show no signs of illness until the last minute and can go downhill fast.

Keep an eye on the DEFRA website to make sure that there are no outbreaks of disease locally. If you have any concerns you should contact your local Animal Health Office or vet for advice.

Micro/mini pigs are not susceptible to any specific diseases because they are small.

Pig First Aid Box:

- **Manuka Honey (for its antiseptic and healing properties)**
- **Tea tree oil (for treating mites/mange)**
- **Terramycin (antibiotic spray available from the vet)**
- **Violet antiseptic spray (available from animal feed suppliers)**
- **Cotton wool**
- **Bandages**
- **Sun cream factor 50**
- **Vet's telephone number**

Training

Gaining your pig's trust

Training is essential if you want your pig to be an active member of your family with acceptable social skills. A piglet with no manners will turn into a disobedient, ill-mannered pig and no-one wants that. Pigs are very food-orientated. Add to that their high level of intelligence and problem-solving abilities, and training becomes a fun and relatively easy task.

Time spent with your pig should be a positive experience for you both. If things are becoming stressful or your pig just isn't in the right mood, leave well alone and try again another time. Keep training sessions short and sweet. Just like a human being, a pig can soon tire of you harping on about the same old thing and lose interest.

The key is patience and persistence. Always reward good behaviour with lots of praise and a treat. Never hit or frighten your pig otherwise it will soon lose trust in you and will not want to behave.

Micro pig owners quickly realise where the expression 'pig-headed' comes from!

'A pig has just as many rights as a man.'

–George Orwell, 1984

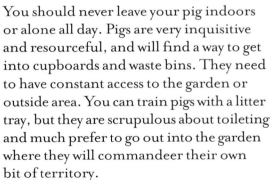

You should never leave your pig indoors or alone all day. Pigs are very inquisitive and resourceful, and will find a way to get into cupboards and waste bins. They need to have constant access to the garden or outside area. You can train pigs with a litter tray, but they are scrupulous about toileting and much prefer to go out into the garden where they will commandeer their own bit of territory.

As they are such intelligent animals, pigs will pick up good toileting habits from your dogs and cats. They will let you know when they need to go outside and will always use the same patch of ground. I have a dog flap fitted in my kitchen door so all the animals can let themselves in and out of the house as they please.

Never leave your pig locked up in the house all day.

Pigs are really good at swimming.

Hand feeding

Hand feeding teaches your piglet to be gentle and not to snatch. It is also a good way to bond, calmly talking to your new pet. It's essential that you both feel relaxed with each other. If your pig snatches food from your hand, a firm 'No biting' is required. Use lots of praise and kind words when your piglet takes the food from you in the proper way. Trust is key: once your pig trusts you, it will listen to your every word.

When training use healthy carrot sticks, grapes and baby sweetcorn as treats.

Come

Teaching your pig to come to you on command is a good starting point. Stand about 1.5m (5ft) away and show your pig the treat you have in your hand. As it walks towards you say, 'Come pig' or use the pig's name. When it arrives, give it the treat and say, 'Good pig,' giving it plenty of praise. You can gradually increase the distance between you and your pig. Soon you will be able to call it from any room in the house.

Teach your pig to recognise its own name and to associate you calling with treats and praise.

Sit

Take a piece of your pig's favourite food and hold it in front of its nose. Raise your hand over its head and its nose will follow, simultaneously forcing its bottom to touch the floor. Once it is sitting, give it its treat and say, 'Sit,' and then repeat the process. Before long it will be sitting on command — it really is that simple!

Biting

All animals can bite when provoked. Their natural reaction is either fear or aggression. If an animal is taught how to behave from an early age, however, nipping should not be a problem in adulthood. If your pig does bite, firmly tell it 'No biting' and don't give it any praise or treats. It is up to the responsible owner to instil discipline and obedience. If your pig is going to be in the house, you have to make rules.

'You should never try and teach a pig to read for two reasons. First, it's impossible; and secondly, it annoys the hell out of the pig!'

–Will Rogers

Destructive behaviour

A bored pig is a destructive pig. Just like children they quickly become unhappy when left to their own devices and cause trouble — usually by rooting through items such as clothing, furniture, plants and carpets. If this is happening you must first attempt to distract your pig from such behaviour. Try giving it its own toys to play with, perhaps an old blanket or towel to push around. You could spend some time with your pet, teaching it to fetch a ball or toy.

Pigs are always looking for something to do and need mental stimulation to keep them from mischief. This is another reason why I recommend getting more than one pig, especially if you don't have other pets.

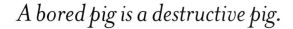

A bored pig is a destructive pig.

Do not constantly give your pig treats as you will just become a food source for it. If this happens it will begin pushing you for more food and this can become rough if not nipped in the bud early.

Try to make sure that your pig does have a little time alone during the day so it can learn to cope in your absence, play with toys and occupy itself when needed.

Discipline

Pigs are like children; they need to be disciplined when bad behaviour is taking place and not afterwards. If you return to a room after a period of absence to find your bin turned over or a poo on the carpet and then punish your pig, it simply will not understand. From the pig's point of view you have just come into the room and started screaming and shouting at it for no good reason. If this happens often it will soon lose trust in its new mummy/daddy. A good stern 'No' directed at your pig is enough to make it think twice about doing it again. Once you own a pig you'll soon understand where phrases like 'stubborn as a pig' and 'pig-headed' came from! You should never hit or punish your pig in an aggressive manner; just move it away from the area and distract it with something new. Treat your pig as you would a puppy — if you reward the good behaviour and ignore the bad, it will soon learn what is expected and become a well-behaved member of the family who is a pleasure to have around.

'I learned long ago, never to wrestle with a pig, you get dirty; and besides, the pig likes it.'

–George Bernard Shaw

Toilet training – inside

Pigs are more than capable of being clean in the house and can be trained either to use a litter tray or ask to be let out into the garden to relieve themselves. Even in the wild they have an area where they always go to 'do their business' and this will be as far away from where they eat and sleep as they can make it.

Perseverance is the key with toilet training. For litter training you will require a shallow litter tray, newspaper to line the tray and perhaps some woodchips or shavings. Don't use cat litter: some pigs will try to eat it, which will upset their stomach. Once the litter tray is set up, don't give your pig the run of the house. Keep your pig in a small area with the tray. If it is given too much space, it will take much longer to get to grips with the fact that this tray is meant to be used as a toilet. If your pig does a poo on the floor, simply transfer the faeces to the litter tray. A pig will soon recognise what the tray is for and will hop in when the need arises. If your pig wants to use a specific area of the room, move the tray there. *Never* place a litter tray near to feeding bowls. Pigs are very fussy animals and will always go as far away from their eating area as possible to relieve themselves.

Pigs are extremely clean by nature.

A top tip for toilet training, used by several pig breeders, is that pigs usually urinate while they are drinking. Place your pig's bowl of water just the other side of the litter tray. It will have to step inside to drink and, with luck, will wee in the tray. Once this has happened a few times, the water bowl can be moved away from the area. Your pig will have learned to use the tray.

Toilet training – outside

When your pig has mastered using the litter tray, you can start moving it very gradually towards the door to indicate that you would like your pet to go outside. Don't just take up the tray and put it outside immediately as this will confuse the pig. If you have a cat or dog flap, your pig may already have discovered how to get out into the garden and be hopping in and out. I would always recommend getting a dog flap. Encourage it to use the cat or dog flap by offering a treat, such as a grape or a piece of carrot, when the pig climbs through. It will soon learn that this is the right thing to do. If you don't have a cat or dog flap, leave the door open a bit with the litter tray outside. Your pig will begin to grasp the idea that, when the door is shut, it needs to ask to leave the room. If it's cold or raining, your pet may need some gentle persuasion. Let your piglet into the garden and when it does its business, reward it with a treat and tell it that it's a good pig.

Even in the wild, pigs will section off special areas of their habitat for sleeping, eating and as a toilet. Their natural instinct is to have the toilet as far away from their eating area as possible. So your pig will probably choose a particular area of your garden as its toilet and stick with it.

Make your pig feel proud of itself. Reward every new achievement: once learned they are never forgotten.

Resources

DEFRA
Helpline: 08459 33 55 77
www.defra.gov.uk/animalhealth

Animal Health Helpline: 0844 88 44 600

Rural Payments Agency
www.rpa.gov.uk

Little Pig Farm
www.thelittlepigfarms.com

Pig Supplies:
www.pigemporium.co.uk

Acknowledgements

Thanks to:

Deborah Roberts, who helped me with this book, let us shoot in her garden, and is the best PA and friend.

Andy Croft and Mo Coleman for being the best brother and sister-in-law in the world.

Ashleigh Read for the lemons.

Kate Whitaker for being such a fabulous photographer. To her and her lovely assistant Raquel for getting down and dirty with the pigs.

Alex and Emma Smith for their wonderful design, jam sandwiches and for letting us play with their Saddlebacks. Their children Lily and Oscar for being great models.

Heather and Rebecca Luff who modelled and let us shoot in their beautiful garden.

James, Susie, Grace and Harriet Adam; Giles, Sarah, Emily, Lulu and Freddie Kane; Andy, Tor, Sophie, Emily and James Sandars for being very willing models and pig keepers for the day.

Kyle Cathie and all in her office for giving me this wonderful opportunity. Especially to Catharine Robertson.

Sue Fox for her great way with words.

Robert Tibbles for looking after the stars of the show.

Everyone at the Isle Veterinary Group, Ely, for looking after the piggies.

Lynne and Malcolm at Malcolm Grimes & Co. for believing in me.

Heidi and Matt Firth for being so supportive (and for the Mojitos!).

Fitch for watching my back.

Peter Green and all at KPM Solicitors.

Ryan Helman for being a true friend.

Skylark Garden Centre, March.

Bearts of Stowbridge for supplying pig feed.

Nigel Bates for looking after the vehicles and taking the pig poo.

Kevin Curson and all at Kevley Marketing for the vegetables.

All of our customers and supporters.

And of course… our beautiful micro pigs!